Good Night, God

Amy Fazzini
Illustrated by Tatiana Prolyaka

Xulon Press
2301 Lucien Way #415
Maitland, FL 32751
407.339.4217

www.xulonpress.com

Unless otherwise indicated, Scripture quotations taken from the Holy Bible, New International Version (NIV). Copyright © 1973, 1978, 1984, 2011 by Biblica, Inc.™. Used by permission. All rights reserved.

Printed in the United States of America

Paperback ISBN-13: 978-1-66284-415-7
Hard Cover ISBN-13: 978-1-66284-494-2
Ebook ISBN-13: 978-1-66284-416-4

As I lay my head down
and before I start to dream,

I thank God for the special things
He does for you and me.

He does so many things for me
that I try to remember.

He fills our days and hearts with love,
like Christmas in December.

He keeps me safe all through the day,
like when I walk to school.

He helps me be so kind to friends
and follow all the rules.

He keeps us safe when in our car
and shopping at the store.

He helps us every morning out
of bed to conquer more.

He makes the birdies in the sky
that sing us all awake.

Don't ever think we let Him down
when making a mistake.

He is so kind and loving
and knows when we do wrong.

We ask Him for forgiveness,
and we keep on marching on.

When it gets all dark outside
and nighttime comes around,

He gives us that great moon above
to lighten up the town.

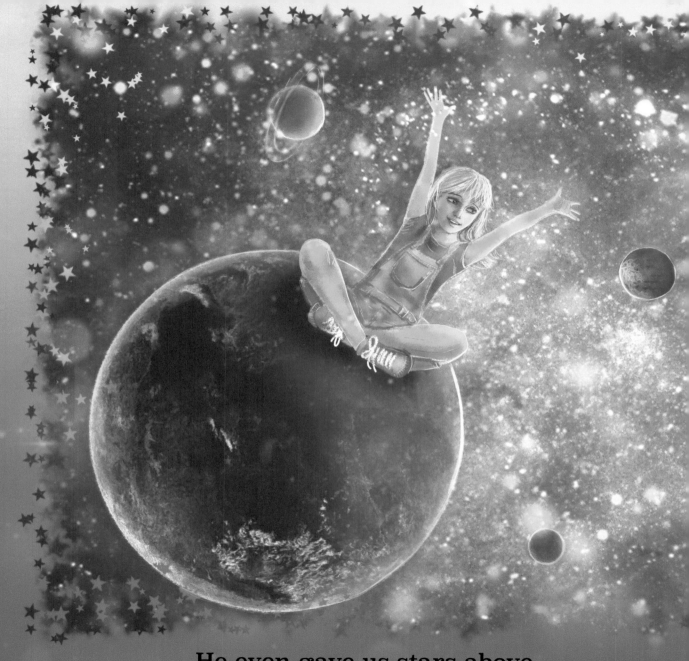

He even gave us stars above
and planets, yes, it's true!

It's just so quite amazing all the
blessings God gives you.

He is so big and cuddly,
like my big teddy bear.

He always listens when I speak,
so I'm never alone anywhere.

As I get all tucked in bed
and all the house is dreaming,

I like to say one more good night
to a God who knows my feelings.

Good night, God in heaven,
I thank you for the day.

Good night and keep me safe and tight
until the next new day.

The Lord watches over you. The Lord is your shade at your right hand; The sun will not harm you by day, nor the moon by night. The Lord will keep you from all harm.

He will watch over your life. The Lord will watch over your coming and going both now and forevermore.

Psalms 121:5-8 (NIV)

CPSIA information can be obtained
at www.ICGtesting.com
Printed in the USA
LVHW070334050422
715321LV00004B/68